A Trip to the Dentist

THIS EDITION

Produced for DK by WonderLab Group LLC
Jennifer Emmett, Erica Green, Kate Hale, *Founders*

Editor Maya Myers; **Photography Editor** Nicole DiMella; **Managing Editor** Rachel Houghton;
Designers Project Design Company; **Researcher** Michelle Harris; **Copy Editor** Lori Merritt;
Indexer Connie Binder; **Proofreader** Susan K. Hom; **Series Reading Specialist** Dr. Jennifer Albro

First American Edition, 2025
Published in the United States by DK Publishing, a division of Penguin Random House LLC
1745 Broadway, 20th Floor, New York, NY 10019

A catalog record for this book is available from the Library of Congress.
HC ISBN: 978-0-5939-6244-2
PB ISBN: 978-0-5939-6243-5
DK books are available at special discounts when purchased in bulk for sales promotions, premiums, fund-raising,
or educational use. For details, contact:
DK Publishing Special Markets, 1745 Broadway, 20th Floor, New York, NY 10019
SpecialSales@dk.com

Printed and bound in China
Super Readers Lexile® levels 310L to 490L
Lexile® is the registered trademark of MetaMetrics, Inc. Copyright © 2024 MetaMetrics, Inc. All rights reserved.

The publisher would like to thank the following for their kind permission to reproduce their images:
a=above; c=center; b=below; l=left; r=right; t=top; b/g=background
Adobe Stock: DN6 14br, Edgar1 BJ 20cr, KDdesignphoto 16; **Dreamstime.com:** Yuri Arcurs 23, Mohammed
Anwarul Kabir Choudhury 17, 30tl, Design56 12cr, Iakov Filimonov 11, 30cl, Ferli Achirulli Kamaruddin 27, Sujit
Kantakat 18, Kamil Macniak 20t, Mikeaubry 25cla, Igor Mojzes 19, Alena Ohneva 21, Pelfophoto 28, Alexander
Pokusay 15, Tina Zovteva 12cl; **Getty Images:** DigitalVision / Thomas Barwick 1; **Getty Images / iStock:**
Dardespot 3, E+ / Aldomurillo 10, E+ / Davidf 9, E+ / Igor Alecsander 29, E+ / Kobus Louw 26,
E+ / ProfessionalStudioImages 7t, E+ / Renata Angerami 7b, E+ / Vesnaandjic 8, JBryson 14bl, 30bl, Mapo 22,
30cla, Peak Stock 24, Mark Swallow 4-5, XiXinXing 13

Cover images: *Front:* **Dreamstime.com:** Dekart001 (Background); Getty Images / iStock: Lacheev;
Back: **Dreamstime.com:** Roman Egorov cra; **Shutterstock.com:** Imhaf Maulana cla, clb

www.dk.com

A Trip to the Dentist

K.E. Lewis

Contents

Going to the Dentist

It's been six months.
It's time to see
the dentist!

A dentist is a doctor who
takes care of your teeth.
Dentists help teeth
stay clean and strong.
They make sure your
gums are healthy.
They can even help get
rid of bad breath!

At the Office

Welcome to the dentist's office!

A receptionist says hello. He shows you where to wait.

Other people are waiting, too. Everyone needs clean, strong teeth!

You're here for a checkup. First, the hygienist will do your cleaning. Then, the dentist will give you an exam.

Soon, someone calls your name. This is the hygienist. A hygienist is trained to clean and check your teeth.

Open Wide!

The hygienist takes you to an exam room.

"Take a seat." They point to a big chair. It's pretty comfy!

They hand you a cool pair of glasses. They clip a paper bib around your neck.

"Open wide!"

You open your mouth.
Look at all those teeth!

The hygienist counts your teeth. Children have 20 primary teeth. These are your first teeth. They poked through your gums when you were a baby. They will all fall out!

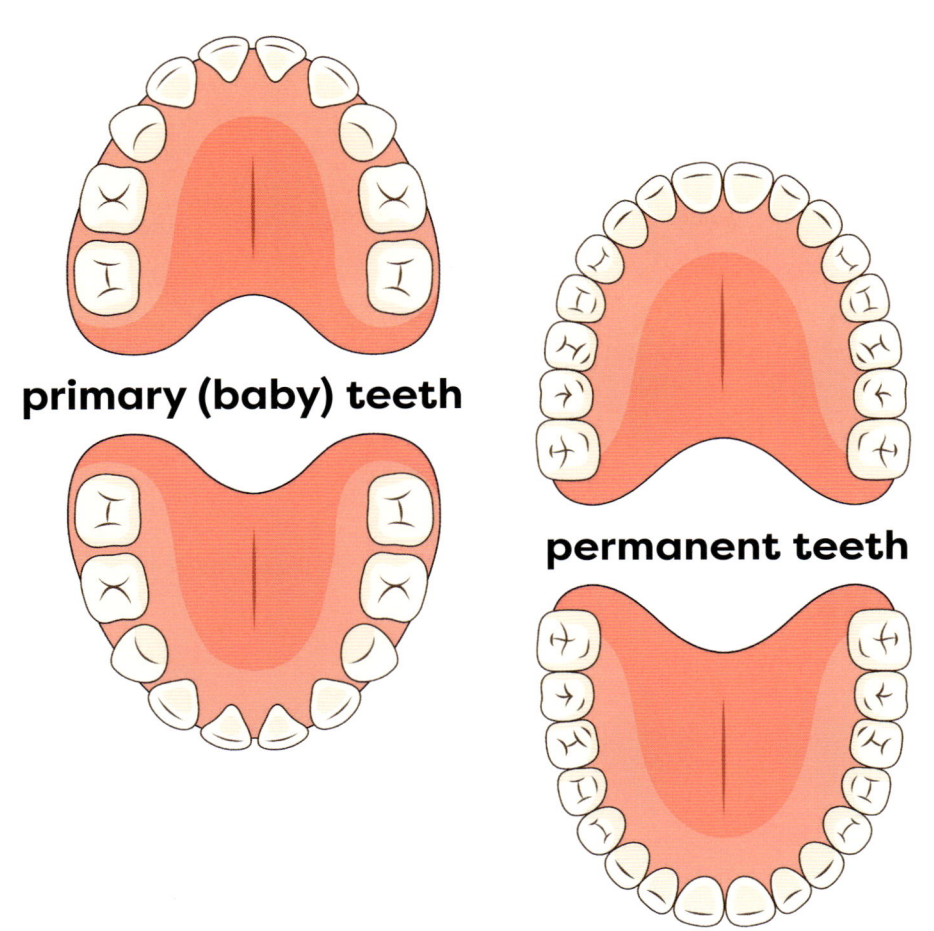

primary (baby) teeth

permanent teeth

But don't worry. Permanent teeth will take their place. You'll have 32 permanent teeth. They should last the rest of your life!

Next, it's X-ray time.

A heavy apron protects your body from the X-ray.

The hygienist puts an X-ray device in your mouth.

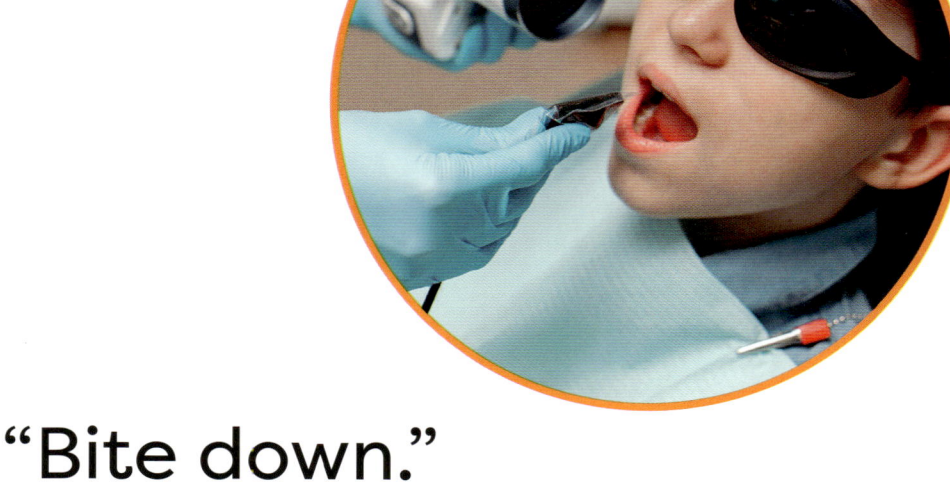

"Bite down."
The hygienist steps out of the room.

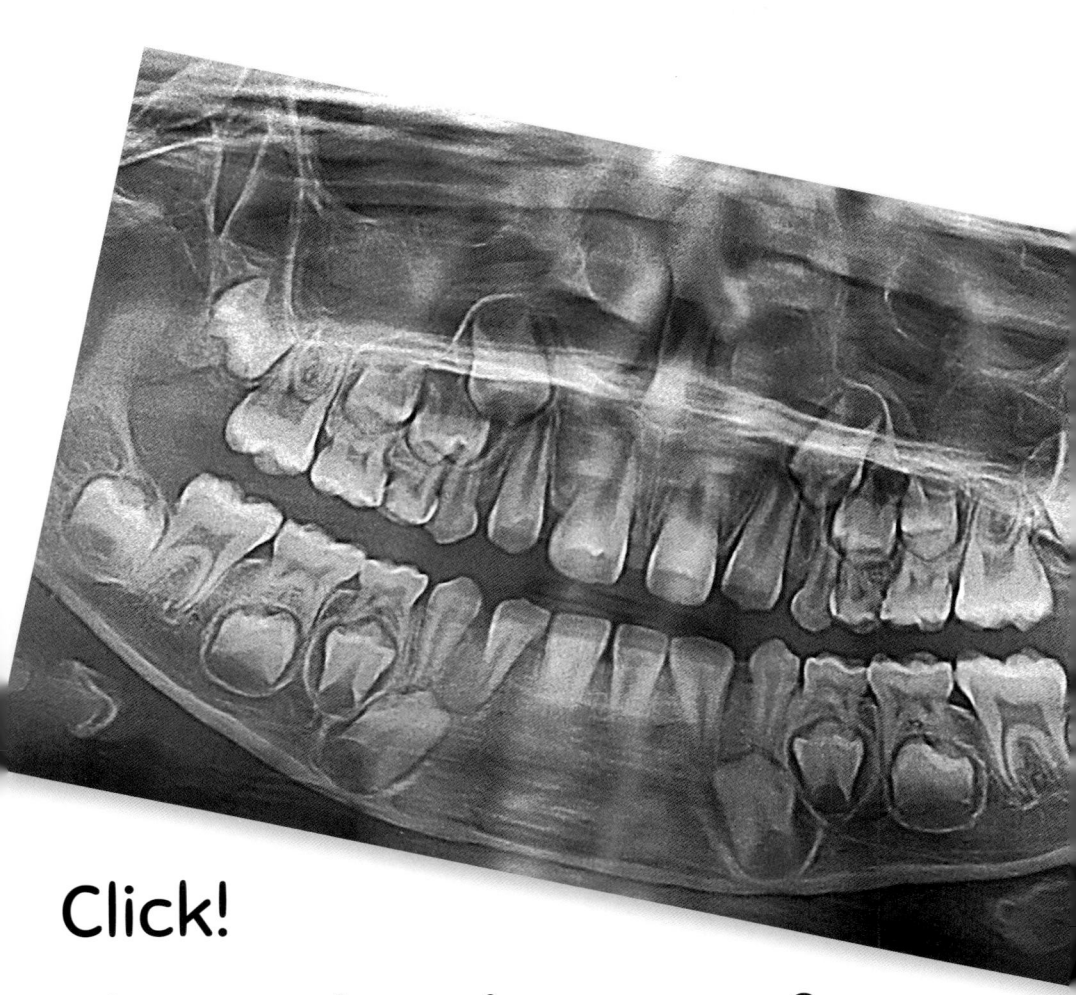

Click!

They take pictures of the teeth and bones in your mouth.

X-rays show the bones under your skin and muscle.

The Cleaning

Now, it's time to get your teeth nice and sparkly!

The hygienist uses special tools. They remove plaque and tartar.

Plaque is a film that builds up on your teeth.

When plaque hardens, it becomes tartar. Tartar is hard to scrape off.

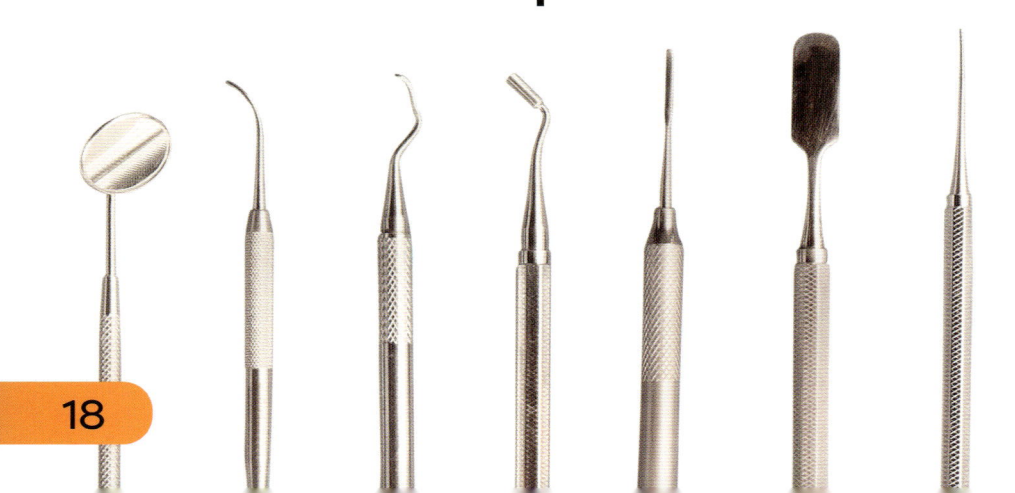

suction wand

The hygienist squirts water into your mouth to rinse it. A suction wand sucks the water back out!

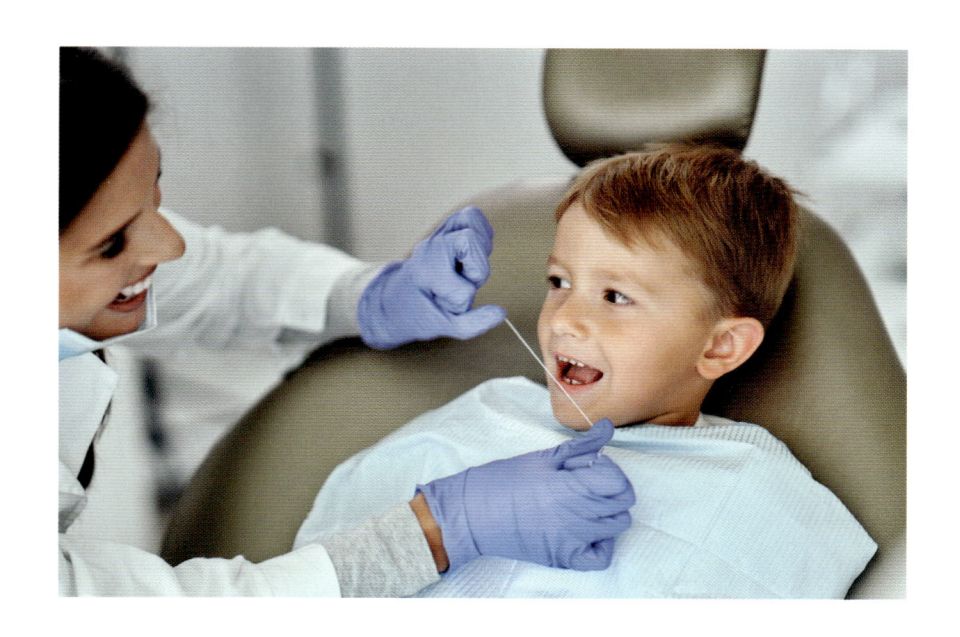

The hygienist uses floss. This cleans between your teeth.

Then, they get a polishing tool. They dip it in a sticky paste.

Rrrrmm. Rrrrmm. Rrrrmm.

Now, rinse and spit!

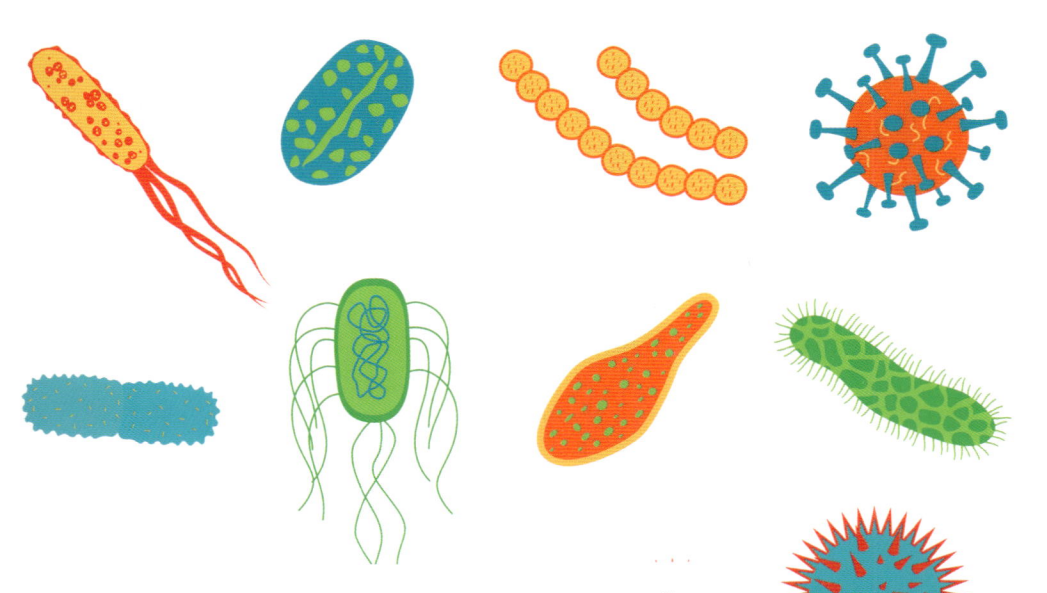

There are around 20 billion bacteria in your mouth!

Some bacteria can cause damage. They can give you bad breath and diseases.

The cleaning removes bad bacteria from your mouth.

The Exam

Now, the dentist comes in. They make sure your teeth are growing well. They use a probe to check your enamel. The enamel is the outer layer of your teeth. It is harder than your bones.

probe

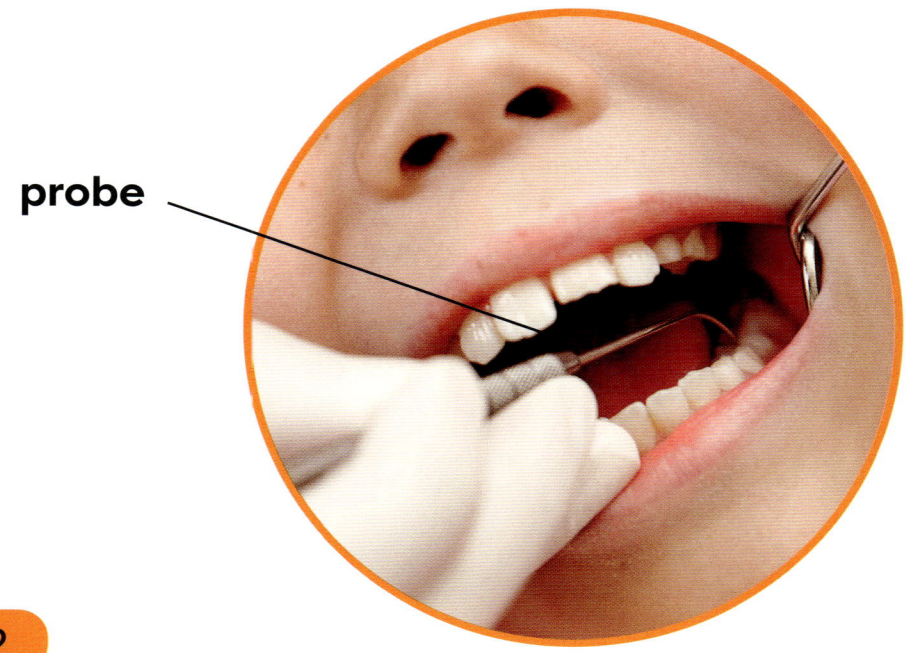

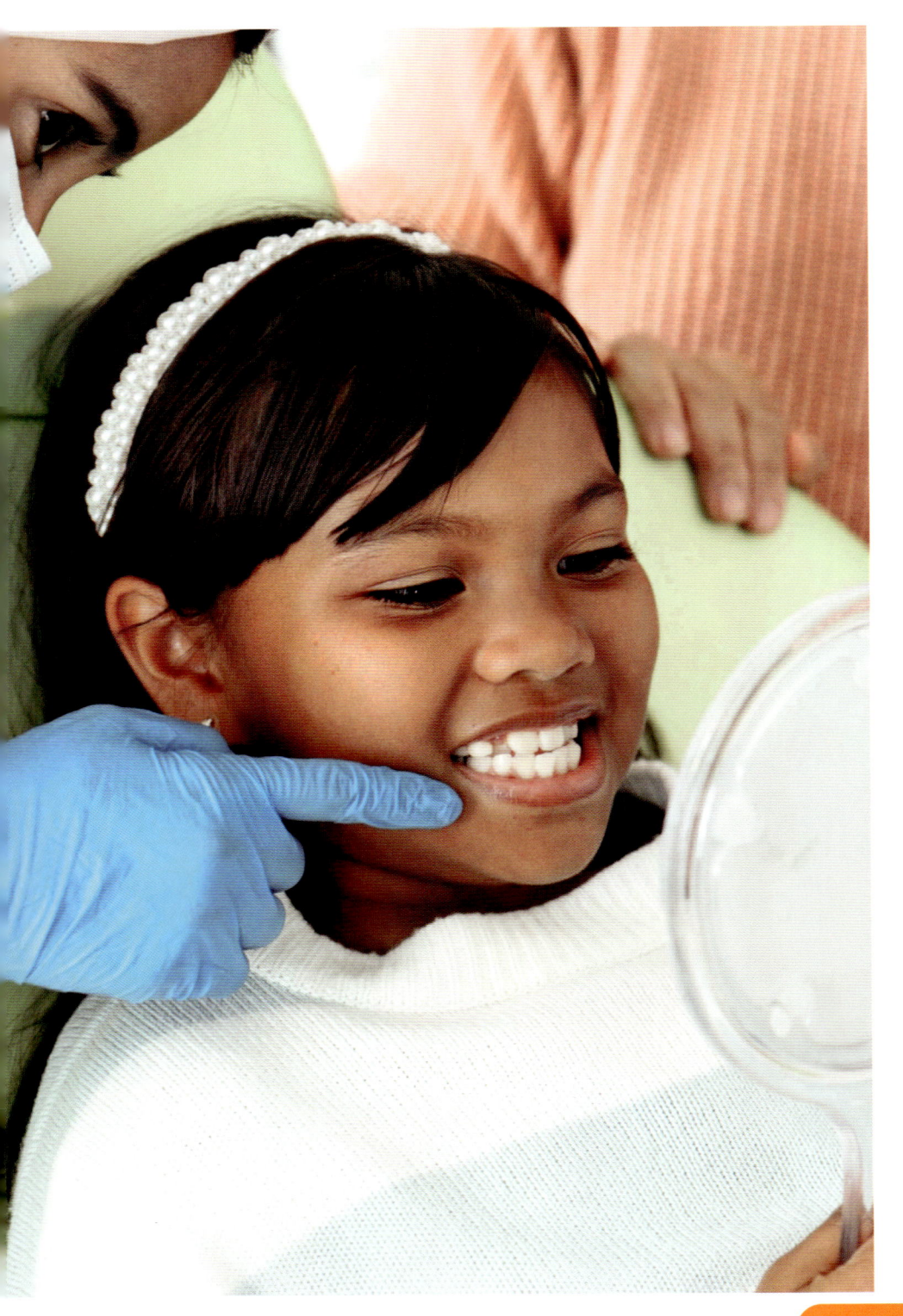

The dentist checks your X-rays.

They look for cavities. A cavity is a hole in your tooth. It can really hurt. Cavities come from plaque and tartar building up on your teeth.

Good thing your teeth are nice and clean now!

How can you reduce plaque?

 Avoid sugary drinks

 Avoid sweets

 Avoid crackers and chips

 Brush and floss regularly

Ready to Shine

You're all done!
The hygienist gives
you a new toothbrush
and a sticker!

They remind you:

"Brush at least twice a day."

"Make sure you floss."

"Be careful what you eat."

In six months, you'll be back.

The receptionist sets a date and time for your next visit.

Time to show the world your sparkling smile.

And keep taking care of those teeth!

Glossary

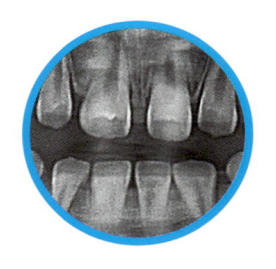
cavity
a hole in a tooth

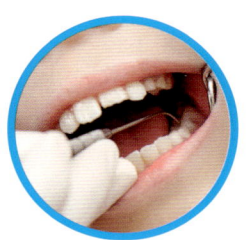
enamel
the outermost layer
of a tooth

hygienist
a person trained to
clean teeth

plaque
the yellowish film that
builds up on teeth

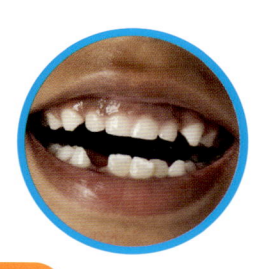
primary teeth
the first set of teeth
humans grow

Index

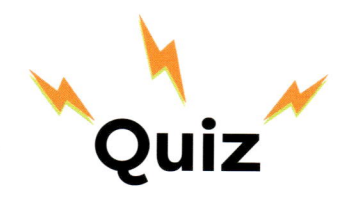

Quiz

Answer the questions to see what you have learned. Check your answers with an adult.

1. True or False: You should go to the dentist every six months.

2. Fill in the blank: The person at the dentist's office who shows you where to wait is called the _____.

3. How many permanent teeth will you have?

4. How many bacteria live in your mouth?

5. Name some things that might make plaque build up on your teeth.

1. True 2. The receptionist 3. 32 4. About 20 billion
5. Sugary drinks, sweets, crackers and chips, not brushing and flossing regularly